FOREWORD BY RUSSELL BRUNSON

Clubhouse

Guidebook For Dentistry

The Ultimate Guide for *Growing your Practice* Through the Hottest New Social App

FOREWORD BY RUSSELL BRUNSON

Clubhouse

Guidebook For Dentistry

The Ultimate Guide for *Growing your Practice* Through the Hottest New Social App

DR. ANISSA HOLMES

CLUBHOUSE GUIDEBOOK FOR DENTISTRY: The Ultimate Guide for Growing Your Practice Through the Hottest New Social App

Library of Congress Cataloging in-Publication Data:

Anissa Holmes

CLUBHOUSE GUIDEBOOK FOR DENTISTRY: The Ultimate Guide for Growing Your Practice Through the Hottest New Social App

ISBN: 978-1-932448-20-7 (Paperback)

Available in Kindle, eBook

Foreword by Russell Brunson

Anissa Holmes is a decade ahead of most professionals in her field. Her ability to see beyond the horizon makes her create realities beyond what the eyes can see. She is an early bird! She shows up early to every game, and she's always first to get the ball rolling.

She was the first dentist with a website and the first to teach people how to use marketing funnels. She figured out how to take several funnel strategies and weave them into an approach that doesn't even look like marketing, but it works!

Recently, my dentist asked me for marketing advice, and my response was, "Do whatever Anissa does; she's the best." When other dentists ask me how to use funnels, I direct them straight to Anissa because, without a doubt, I know they are in good hands. She loves to help people, but she never forgets the bigger picture—getting more patients in the door (and she never forgets those in her back pocket). So, when Clubhouse came on the scene . . .

She showed up . . .

She checked it out . . . and leveraged the opportunity by building her strategy.

Now, she's winning on the Clubhouse stage, while it is still hot!

The Clubhouse space is a catalyst for entrepreneurial development. At its core is conversation, which is the driver behind every marketing strategy. That said, Clubhouse creates a superb opportunity for entrepreneurship through communication. Almost everyone can make a sale via a marketing strategy, no matter how small. However, true entrepreneurship is building a tribe of people who buys into you repeatedly and sticks with you over the long haul.

When we built **ClickFunnels**, we wanted to do more than build software; we wanted to build something that would foster a relationship with our customers. We wanted to make the connection, add value and create a lifelong following. Professionals in business are often good at getting people to work and customers to come in the door. However, as they create new customers, they forget to build a movement that continues to adds value.

The Clubhouse app is perhaps the most efficient vehicle to create a tribe that sticks with you over the long haul.

Anissa identified this and has done precisely that.

The extraordinary thing about Clubhouse is that it's similar to traditional marketing (pre-internet); when we go to all those Business Network International (BNI) meetings. Yes! Clubhouse is like the quick equivalent of what the Chamber of Commerce was back in the day. You showed up and networked to get clients and connect with other influencers in the local market.

It's different now, especially post-COVID. People were forced to stop meeting in person, and immediately, Clubhouse came with a digital solution for connection at the industry level. With Clubhouse, we get to:

- meet other people who are doing what we're doing;
- learn best practices;
- remain current;
- connect with local communities; and
- form lasting patient service-relationships.

Now is the time to get in!

Some people will smack themselves when it's too late, looking back and saying, "I could have been at the beginning of it, but I missed it because I was not paying attention."

Anissa has crafted another winning strategy that shows you how to add value and succeed on Clubhouse. Right now, you have a guide that makes it easy to start. Right here, you have a map that shows you the ways to succeed at the beginning of the trend and not at the end.

The CLUBHOUSE GUIDEBOOK FOR DENTISTRY is easy to understand and simple to action. This book is the map that will get you to meet more clients, do better networking, build better client relationships, and get you to master the HOTTEST NEW SOCIAL APP. The cake beneath the icing is the value-added in the learning sessions with other dentists.

In the past, getting access to influencers in your space was expensive. Now you can forget about the expense and focus on understanding the strategies that will get you chased by success. This book will give you all the tactics help you understand the opportunity, and show you step by step how to execute them.

Join Clubhouse, get into rooms, network with the people who have had the most successes inside your market, and don't let go of this book!

Cheers,

Russell Brunson

CH: @RussellBrunson

P.S. See you on there!

Dedication

Consider this a written invitation and pre-welcome party to the Clubhouse Dentists' family!

If you long for that professional connection, conversation and collaboration, this book is dedicated to you!

If you miss those moments of professional bonding around the fire pit, then this book is definitely dedicated to you!

Why?

Well, when the reality of the pandemic sunk in, and I realized the impact on our industry, I wondered how you were coping. So, when I found the place that would revive those fire pit nights that connected our families and our businesses, I had to get you in without hesitation.

For a moment, I wondered if it would be inappropriate to dedicate it to the ones who understood the value of people and the power of words. Tradition would dictate that this book be dedicated to family and friends. But they would not quite get it. So, I thought, what the heck . . . it's for you, the professional dentist, and those I serve in the fraternity.

I have one more invitation for you . . .

I invite you to embrace this dedication and allow the value added to move you to connect with those of us already on Clubhouse. Let it pull you into discussions and give you that fulfillment of making someone smile again. Own it and receive the opportunities the community provides. Then, get ready for abundant growth and business success!

Cheers,

Dr. Anissa Holmes

CH: @AnissaHolmes

Acknowledgments

I acknowledge God, first and foremost, for guiding me along and never leaving my side.

Thanks to my kids, Ana and Brady; they mean the world to me. I know they are literally going to change the world!

From a heart full of gratitude, I say thank you to Sara, Tammy, and Dr. Keisha Smith-Pagan, for always supporting me and my vision and helping me make an impact in the world.

Thank you to Elijah, who has seen my highs and lows and always encouraged me to think bigger. Your friendship means the world to me.

Last but not least, thank you to my mentor, Russell Brunson, who taught me just about everything I know about marketing. Your funnel is our hourglass.

Thank you, my dream team!

Show Up And Take Action

Showing up is one thing, but taking action raises the bar!

If you registered for a conference, booked your ticket, prepared your luggage, showed up, and then realized you left your business cards on your desk at the office, what would you do to secure connections?

I have seen this happen to several colleagues, but the best solution is to show up, share valuable information, and invite new connections to direct messages for a freebie.

As a dentist, I have been blessed with several wisdom-teaching experiences that have catalyzed my growth in the industry. I am one from the trenches, building my practice and helping others grow. However, never have I seen a better avenue to connect, learn, share and grow than the opportunity the Clubhouse app affords.

I thought it was important to write this book because I know that (from a marketing standpoint) showing up early and taking action together will get us ahead faster.

Back in 2001, when websites just started, I was very excited. At that time, dentists could use a practice management software called Dentrix to build their websites. I thought it was a fantastic opportunity, so I grabbed it with both hands. I was so elated that I registered a domain name and created the first dentist website.

The opportunity expanded the boundaries of my business. I had just started my practice, and before I knew it, I was catapulted into a reality other only dreamt of living.

A few things happened:

Number one, my website was selected to represent websites in the dental industry. I remember walking into the Henman Dental meeting in Atlanta and seeing my practice's website all over the exhibition hall.

Number two, which was even more powerful was that my website was at the top of the result page of Google's "dental related" searches. That gave me an early comer's advantage. What advantage? The advantage of **not** investing time and enormous sums of money to optimize and leverage my presence online. I got it for free, simply by showing up first, where others were yet to be seen.

My first practice was in Birmingham. When I moved to another city, the same thing happened. I was there first, and the results showed in the many people I served and the smiles I created. And yes, the same thing recurred everywhere I took my practice, even on Facebook.

When Facebook came on the scene, I was in the process of building another startup practice. I was so excited, my team and I leveraged Facebook for this new venture, and before we knew it, we had 50,000 people following my Facebook page.

If I tried to do the same thing today, it would be challenging to grow a following, let alone keep them engaged. Nonetheless, I continue to reap benefits via the Facebook page because I showed up first. Additionally, with so many people following us on Facebook, our marketing cost is **close to zero**.

So, when Clubhouse came on the scene, I was one of the first (again) to join. Seeing Clubhouse, my mind immediately went back to the days when I created my website and used Facebook to leverage my practice. I remembered how showing up first helped me and others to grow professionally and profitably.

Yes, Clubhouse was finally here, and I was beyond excited. If you asked me, I was super - duper - supercalifragilisticexpialidocious excited! Why? Because I am a podcaster (There's a story behind that too, perhaps I'll share it later.) and joining Clubhouse was like the best of all worlds coming together.

Clubhouse is a podcast on steroids, but 100% organic and authentic!

While podcasting is a way to connect, share and learn from each other, Clubhouse is a podcast on steroids, 100% organic and authentic! On a podcast, people give information, but on Clubhouse, you can listen, ask questions, and get them answered live and direct, in real-time!

Joining Clubhouse is a uniquely effective way to grow our dental practices. When we join Clubhouse, we are not just a part of a community; we become known in the community. It is a space to build relationships and trust as we serve our communities and grow our businesses. This means we have access to invaluable learning, a supportive community, and the advantage of low customer acquisition cost.

Joining Clubhouse will significantly benefit your business no matter when you show up, but getting there early still has many perks.

I've never seen a platform like this, which allows us to market our practices and grow our businesses, all at the same time. To do this at such an exponentially fast pace is only possible through a like-minded community, connecting, communicating, and collaborating. Clubhouse has transformed my business into more than a service. My practice has a culture of quality **service through relationships**. That's why I am soooo excited about Clubhouse.

Now, here's why I decided to write the Clubhouse Guidebook for Dentistry. When I joined Clubhouse, I realized that it was difficult to find other dental professionals on the app. Of course, I'm an early adopter, which led me to create awareness about the app in my Facebook group. I remember speaking at the Jumpstart conference with other dental coaches and consultants about Social Media. During that session I encouraged them all to get to understand the power of Clubhouse.

I shared that Clubhouse presented the opportunity to create a space where dental professionals could connect, have meaningful discussions and collaborate. That led me to create the first club for dentists on Clubhouse. We needed a space to grow our practices, talk about clinical topics, discuss practice management, marketing, innovations, and technology, all in one place. There we would share in a way where we can hear from authorities, collaborate as users of products, and engage in thought-provoking and value-adding conversations. Now, our Clubhouse dentists club is an ideal space of like-minded professionals with a common goal to listen, learn, serve, and grow our businesses.

That's not all. I wrote this book because I want to share tips and insights on how you could use the Clubhouse app to grow your practice in record time. So, you have time to do more of what you love—making smiles!

Ultimately, you will serve more people, establish more service relationships and watch your business make more money.

Table Of Contents

Chapter 1
What The Heck Is Clubhouse?

Clubhouse is an audio-only social app that allows people to host and join conversations with other users.

Created by co-founders Paul Davison and Rohan Seth, Clubhouse is designed to bring a community of like-minded people together. It connects in real-time, facilitates real conversations, and enables collaborations on real ideas.

Themed Rooms

Clubhouse allows you to create themed rooms to enhance the club or house experience, making it easy for you to listen and have conversations with people on topics of common interests, passions, and pursuits.

Invite-only, iPhone-only

Though already a win in so many respects, Clubhouse is still not yet public. Since its inception, the app has been invite-only and iPhone-only. Based on what I have read, plans are in the pipeline to make Clubhouse available on Android and eventually open the doors so anybody can join. Despite its exclusivity, Clubhouse already has millions of members, including major players in Silicon Valley, celebrities, entrepreneurs, etc.

All Ears on Deck

The exclusivity does not stop there; Clubhouse takes listening to the next level. Not only is the app audio-only, but it is also a no-video and no-recording zone. This means when I am there, I am all ears. Clubhouse understands the power of the present, and members learn to pay close attention to capture the value-added. The best part is that you do not have to stay on the Clubhouse screen to participate in a discussion. As long as you don't exit the app, you can still listen-in, share tips, and ask questions.

The app's audio-only feature allows users to listen from anywhere, while doing anything, without the worry of video or the need for typing. Trust me; I have caught myself a few times taking my phone into the bathroom to continue listening to a panel discussion.

Chapter 2
Why Clubhouse For Dental Professionals?

As a community of dental professionals going through a pandemic together, we have realized how much we crave being around the fire pit—at a dental conference, with the freedom to share, learn and collaborate. We want to talk about the newest technology and the perils of the new materials we use in our practices. We also crave sitting together at a table, talking about what we are doing to get patients.

The Clubhouse app satisfies that yearning. It stimulates the desire to help others and gratifies in a way our anticipation could not have conceived. It is the power of people. Clubhouse is that fire pit that highlights how much life is about people and the power that resides in a community!

Clubhouse will change your life and your business northwards. It will get you there in real-time, fast, and with a community to support you.

More and more people are joining Clubhouse daily. They join to get information about business management, health, starting a YouTube channel, real estate, accounting, copywriting, dentistry, product marketing, and much more. Since Clubhouse is the place where people now go to learn, listen and connect, then there is no better place for us to

- grow our community (of dentist professionals);
- stay industry current;
- help each other;
- provide information to patients;
- market our practices;
- get patients; and
- teach and learn.

At Clubhouse, we get to connect, have conversations and collaborate. I like to call them "the 3Cs of Clubhouse."

You Get to Connect: The app is a connector, but not in the usual way. It forgets about the seating count, the décor, and the file folders. You simply need to show up, listen, learn, share and grow. By creating rooms, joining, and participating in events, you get to connect with like-minded people and learn from them. The connections you make on Clubhouse will drive you to be better, then elevate you to being the best at what you do.

I've been in Clubhouse rooms where a group of dentists connected with old dental schoolmates to discuss industry matters. I had the opportunity to connect with students I talked with while in college; now, we moderate panels together on topics of mutual interest. Some are not dental professionals, but they provide business knowledge to persons in the medical field.

Creating a weekly event on Clubhouse is one of the ways you get to connect with others. You can create a room where people get to listen and learn from you. Of course, these same persons are going to book services with you as well. They will find you on other social media platforms and even direct message (DM) you to continue a conversation. That's the power of the Clubhouse connection right there.

You Get to Have Conversations: After you've made connections, your next step is to have those meaningful conversations where you share, listen, and learn. They also provide that superb opportunity to prove yourself as the authority in your space. Providing expert information to patients and helping other dentists allows you to become the expert, teacher, or coach on a particular subject. Whether it is about treating a broken tooth or starting a new practice, there are people on Clubhouse ready to listen and learn from you.

You Get to Collaborate: What I and perhaps others may not have realized (when we joined) is the fantastic opportunity to collaborate with other professionals. The community environment on Clubhouse allows us to partner with dental professionals and even other medical professionals on business activities. For example, we can host educational events to teach and spread awareness of our services.

On Clubhouse, I join discussions as a listener, coach, and speaker. I am pleased about this because together, I get to help my colleagues grow faster. The connections we make will foster collaborative opportunities between us as professionals, eventually growing our businesses. The app is about connecting a community. Let's use that power to support each other and grow our industry.

Since I joined Clubhouse, I have had multiple huge dental companies reach out to me to partner on projects and speak at their events, all as a result of hearing me on CLUBHOUSE!!!

***

Fast Growth on Clubhouse

Growing on Clubhouse is like growing on steroids! Making connections through Clubhouse will enable you to:

- build collaborations offline;
- get more patients;

- expand your current business; and
- be recognized as an expert in the industry (teaching or coaching).

Not only will you grow personally, but you will also develop professionally. Clubhouse allows you to be the learner, listener, and expert or learner learning from the expert, all in the same event. In years past, we've had to pay tens of thousands of dollars to learn. Now, every day, I sit in a room listening, learning, taking lurked notes, for FREE, thanks to Clubhouse!

Obviously, I am very excited about the app, and besides my early-adopter enthusiasm, Clubhouse is something that we all need to embrace.

Again, for those who choose to be early adopters, we're going to get there early, and our practices will grow faster.

Chapter 3
Predictions For Our Industry

Many industries, businesses, and even platforms have remarkably pivoted in response to the global shutdown of 2020. At that point, the realities of the worldwide pandemic influenced the invention of many necessary solutions. Clubhouse falls in the middle of being defined as an essential invention and a welcomed solution. It created a space for strategic discussion to continue and the revolution of connecting, collaborating, and growing at a higher level with higher value, for less.

Clubhouse will become the #1 social app for us to connect, collaborate and build our businesses.

Not only are all industries represented on Clubhouse, but experts and elites are also taking the lead to help others via the app. Digital marketers, industry professionals, celebrities, experts, and even investors have become housemates. Without a doubt, Clubhouse will become the:

- leading platform and strategy for getting new patients (including patients who are ready for immediate treatment without discounting);
- platform that builds stronger collaborative alliances;
- platform that creates the best avenues for offline collaborations (locally/internationally);
- social media platform that will surpass the popularity of Facebook groups; and the
- preferred space for online conferences. Clubhouse created a culture of adding value without hassle. It allows you to join easily, listen and learn a lot from anywhere while remaining in your space and in your skin: no makeup, no "hair up," and no "suit up." All focus is on the voice and content!

Chapter 4
How To Use Clubhouse To Get Patients?

Very soon, joining Clubhouse will become one of the leading strategies to grow businesses. The dental industry is already in on the action, and I think it's time you join. Dental health is everybody's business and every dentist's business. Got it?

As soon as you join and start sharing on Clubhouse, you are guaranteed to see the benefits. Your contribution to discussions will create new followers for you, not to mention if you start your rooms or clubs. Soon, you will become the go-to-person for the best answers, best recommendations, and best results. Before you know it, you will be a trusted professional, gaining more patients and professional associations daily. Perhaps you will even open a few more practices and go to market with a new dental product. (Dreams can become a reality)!

But first, how do you make connections and get patients? There are several strategies, some of which I am presently testing. Of course, as we continue to use the app and as it evolves, many other techniques will appear. Here are my suggestions for using Clubhouse to get patients:

- **Connect with People Who Are in Your Local Community**

The best way to do that is to put your location in your biography (bio). When creating your bio, you will have the opportunity to talk about who you are, what you do, and where you are located. Therefore, if you are from Atlanta, it would be best to say you are a dentist in Atlanta. Also, include your specialties and the services that you offer. Clubhouse is a search engine in itself, so stating your location becomes a keywording strategy for search engine optimization (SEO). The keyword "Atlanta" will allow others using that keyword to find and connect with you.

- **Make Sure That You're Connecting with People Who Are on Your Phone Contact List**

First, ensure that your friends who are on Clubhouse are recorded in your phone contact list. Follow them when you join, and hopefully, they will follow you as well. This strategy will allow them to get notifications when you open a room on Clubhouse.

- **Follow Persons Who Join Your Rooms**

This strategy will allow you to expand your network based on common interests. It creates opportunities for more connections. Your followers are notified when you start or join a room. They will be inclined to join, listen and invite others to the room.

- **Leverage Clubs**

Dr. Lee Smith specifically created a club for people who are in Atlanta. That is because joining Clubhouse clubs is a great way to network and find patients. Therefore, make sure you join groups in your area that identify with your business or your interests. Once you join a club, other followers and club members will be able to view your bio and decide if they want to follow you and book your services.

Joining a club also allows you to participate as a club member or follower. Persons will get to hear you and see that you are a dentist in Atlanta. They will be motivated to follow you, again, building your network and reach for patients.

- **Leverage Rooms through Clubs**

Leveraging clubs also helps to grow the audience in your room. For example, as a part of the Atlanta network, you can leverage that keyword by titling your room as "Get your questions asked about children's dentistry, Atlanta." or "Kids' teeth in Atlanta." Now, everybody in Atlanta will see the title and join the room. Also, a notification is sent to your followers, and the connection cycle continues.

- **Keyword Your Bio, and Rooms**

Keywording is so essential; it must be a point all by itself. If you want to be invited to other clubs for a particular area of interest (e.g., small business owner, coach, root canals, kids teeth and dental care, Atlanta dentist), put the word/term in your profile a few times. When people with similar interests search for that keyword, your profile will be in the top results. This strategy helps you to gain authority in that niche.

- **Open an Invitation to Your Room**

If your room is for a specific locale (e.g., Atlanta), ask persons in your room to invite people in Atlanta to have a healthy discussion. The purpose of the conversation is to make you the resource for answers and dental information for the people in Atlanta.

- **Be the Source of Information and Value to Others**

The purpose of the room is to facilitate the discussion. The purpose of the discussion is for you to be established as a resource and an expert. People always have questions about dentistry, so doing a Question & Answer segment as part of the discussion is a perfect way to help people.

- **Invite People in the Room to Follow You**

While you lead the discussion in your room and people are inviting (pinging) people in, prompt them to click on your profile and hit the notification bell. By hitting the bell, they will be notified anytime you talk. Every time you open your rooms (whether every evening or every week), Clubhouse notifies them.

Link your social media handles and contacts to your profile.

Currently, Clubhouse allows you to link only your Twitter and Instagram accounts to your profile. Perhaps by the time you get to read this book, Clubhouse's messaging system might already be out, or at least in progress. Wouldn't that be a treat!

Pro Tip:

Host a weekly room to share valuable information about common dental topics. You can discuss "What to do when you have a missing tooth;" "Q & A - Dentistry for kids;" "How to fit dentistry into your budget," etc. The possibilities are endless.

Chapter 5
How To Join Clubhouse

Invitation Only

At the time of writing this book, Clubhouse is still an invite-only platform. That means, to join, you must be invited by a current member. The app is currently only available to iPhone users. In a town hall meeting, the founders mentioned that they were actively working on the Android version. Perhaps by the second edition of this book, Clubhouse may be available for Android downloads!

A Smart Invite Hack

A cool way to prompt a friend to send you an invite is by downloading the app on your phone to reserve your username. Once that is done, persons who have you on their contact lists will be notified that you are on the waitlist to join Clubhouse.

For example, once I downloaded the Clubhouse app, my good friend @alicialyttle saw that I was on the waitlist. So, she sent me an invite, and I was in! Alicia Lyttle is a speaker, coach, and digital marketer. She helps people build successful online businesses.

New Clubhouse members get only one invite. Invites can only be issued to person in your phone contacts. Therefore, be sure to add your friends to your phone contacts before downloading the app so that you can get one of the scarce Clubhouse invites. Thankfully, over time a person's participation on the app can earn them more invites.

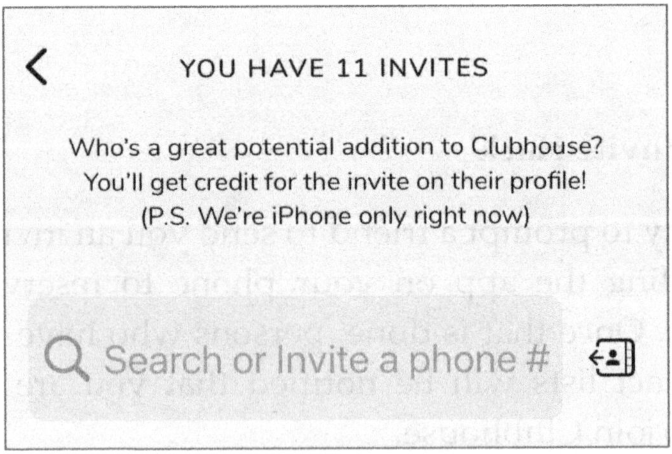

Chapter 6
The Secrets To Setting Up A Killer Profile That Stands Out On Clubhouse

They say you only get one chance to make an excellent first impression. Well, for some Clubhouse members, the second time's the charm. On Clubhouse, a person's first impression of you is more likely to be via your voice. However, once they hear your voice, your profile is next. If there was a way to tell when someone views your profile on Clubhouse, I can almost guarantee you that it would show high viewing when you are on stage in a room.

(*The stage is the section in a room where speakers are shown*)

Your profile is a summary of what you want others to know about you. It sets the tone of who you are and establishes you in the space. Beginning with your profile photo, different sections form your profile. Let's discuss some practical tips for setting up a killer profile.

Profile Photo

Use a profile photo that will make you stand out. You can use one from your archives or take a new photo. Feel free to use an image of you in your practice. That will encourage persons to view your bio. Whatever image you choose, be sure to

- show your best you;
- use a photo that shows your face clearly;
- use a photo with a bright background. One that contrasts nicely with your clothes or hair color; and
- choose a photo that looks great in various sizes.

Guess what? - You can change your profile photo as many times as you like.

Here's my profile photo at the time of writing this book.

Search Engine Optimized (SEO) Profile

The difference between a profile and an SEO profile is the difference between a luxury car and a luxury car with the right fuel. To SEO your profile means you put it in front of more persons because it shows up earlier in search results.

Use these SEO hacks when you set up your Clubhouse profile:

- Keyword by adding your location to the first lines of your bio. (Example, "Cosmetic Dentists in Phoenix")
- Keyword your profile by including topics you have selected as interests. By using appropriate keywords, you are easily found and invited to other clubs.

Your Bio

Your bio is where you get to say what you want others to know about you. Note, the first three lines of your Clubhouse bio are the first lines others get to see before choosing to read more. For example, if you want people to know that you are a dentist in Atlanta, Phoenix, etc., make sure you open your bio by saying (for example) "Cosmetic Dentist in Phoenix."

Crafting Speakers, Coaches, and Consultants Clubhouse Bios

Notice in my bio that I have included that, *"I am a dentist, a coach, and a practice growth expert"* in the first three lines.

Often, people only read what is in the first three lines of the bio because that is what is first displayed. Therefore, I needed to put the information I absolutely wanted everyone to know in the first three lines.

Note, you attract and maintain followers by sharing appropriate activities with them. For example, I have a marketing challenge, so I added the link for persons to access the challenge via my profile.

- **Put in Past and Future Collaborations**

If you hope to share in collaborative work, say it by inviting persons to contact you for help with dental practice marketing, social media marketing, etc. In my bio, I asked persons to message to discuss strategies to help their practice grow.

If you've been featured on different dental publications, add that as well.

If you are a coach, state what type of help you provide, so listeners in a room will match you with their specific needs.

- **Swap Your Bios**

What happens if you are a practicing dentist and you also sell real estate?

Show me someone today who is doing only one thing. No one. It's not new for us dentists to be serving in various ways. It's in our DNA. Perhaps you are the dentist with a real estate company, and you are not sure how to craft a profile that says it all. Not to worry, Clubhouse allows you to create multiple profiles.

Clubhouse permits you to create more than one profile instead of creating combined profiles that say everything. That keeps the profile concise and niched.

From your Note app on your phone, you can create multiple profiles and switch your profiles based on your conversation. For example, if you join a dental room as an expert in Atlanta, your original dental profile will show up.

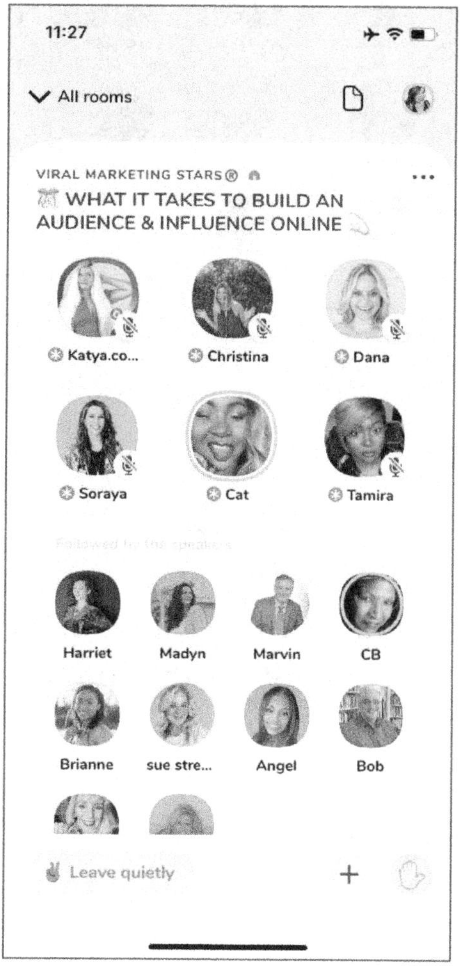

Alternatively, if you join a real estate room as an expert, you can switch to your real estate profile. Love it!

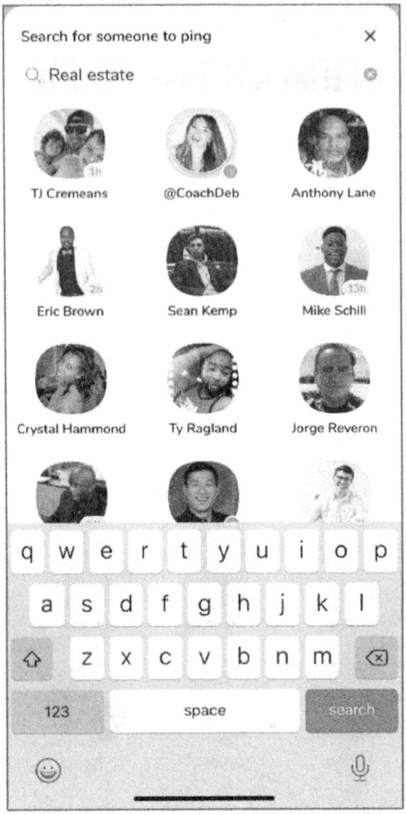

Clubhouse does not stop there; the app also allows you to select your ping audience. As a dentist in a real estate room, you can send a ping to get the opinions of only persons interested in real estate.

To ping only persons interested in real estate, select the plus icon at the bottom of the room page.

Then, type real estate in the search window. Only persons who are interested in real estate will receive your ping.

Again, the power of Clubhouse!

Here are some other essential things to consider when crafting your bio:

- Share who you are and how you help people.
- Use power words to highlight your skills and value.
- Use emojis to separate sections of your profile. They are super fun, and they create flow in the content (e.g., use the tooth emoji). On Clubhouse, emojis are a cool tool; they are searchable, and they make your profile pop. I used the tooth emoji next to the word "Dentist" in my profile.
- In your expanded bio, list some of your accomplishments.
- If you have received awards, done presentations, or hope to do presentations and collaborations, go ahead and add that. (For example, "Contact me for collaborations. I will be delighted to share my knowledge at your dental event.")
- Include a strong call-to-action (CTA). For example, "connect with me at (your Instagram/ Facebook handle)."
- Keep it concise.
- Check your spelling and grammar.

Chapter 7
Profile Photo Hack For Dentists

Changing your profile photo on Clubhouse is easy. You can do this by selecting the image you prefer from your phone. Here are a few cool hacks to make your photo stand out in every room!

Photo Background Hack

I wanted my profile photo to pull others in, so I used https://www.remove.bg/ to remove a busy background. Then I downloaded a free design tool (www.canva.com). I uploaded my image to canva.com and selected a circular frame that made my image pop. Go ahead and update your photo background. Your photo will stand out, and others will notice when you enter a room.

Canva.com also allows you to put more than one photo in a single image. It is a great tool to display before and after photos in one image.

Photo Hack for a Dentist's Profile

Since I found out that I could change my profile photo as often as I wanted, I changed my profile image based on my presentation or the room.

For example, if you are in a room as a dental expert presenting in a dental room, you could change your profile photo to a more clinical one, saved on your phone. If you are presenting on veneers, dental implants, cosmetic dentistry, Invisalign, or even changing silver fillings to white fillings, you could use a before/after image. Once you have changed the profile photo, ask your audience to pull down on their phone screen to refresh the display. On Clubhouse, we call it lingual pull. Once done, they will see the new image.

Engaging Photo Hack by Elijah Desmond

I learned this hack from my good friend, Elijah Desmond. It was a terrific way to engage his audience while he presented in a room. He asked his audience to go to Google and type in the word "red." He then asked them to save a red image to their phones and then change their profile image to the red image whenever they agreed with what the presenter said. Can you imagine all reds when you are presenting? Just awesome!

Ask to Speak Photo Hack

Instead of raising their hand, engage your audience by instructing them to change their profile photo to an "I'd like to speak" photo. I have seen this done in some rooms where the moderator identifies and allows the person on stage by way of their profile image.

As the room gets bigger, the "I'd like to speak" profile photo is a quick and easy way for the moderator to know who wants to come on stage and ask a question. Again, as the app evolves, we will identify more creative ways to leverage the profile photo feature's flexibility.

Have fun creating multiple photos, so you can use these hacks to add value to your Clubhouse experience when next you present, moderate, or listen.

Chapter 8
How Clubhouse Works (The Walk-Through)

As an early adopter, I've always had the privilege to be one of the first to navigate some of the popular social media platforms. Facebook was my first, but without a doubt, Clubhouse is super easy to navigate and get used to.

Here is an easy walk-through to get you started and participating.

After you join Clubhouse and log in for the first time, you are brought to the "Hallway." The Hallway screen displays a menu bar at the top and one at the bottom.

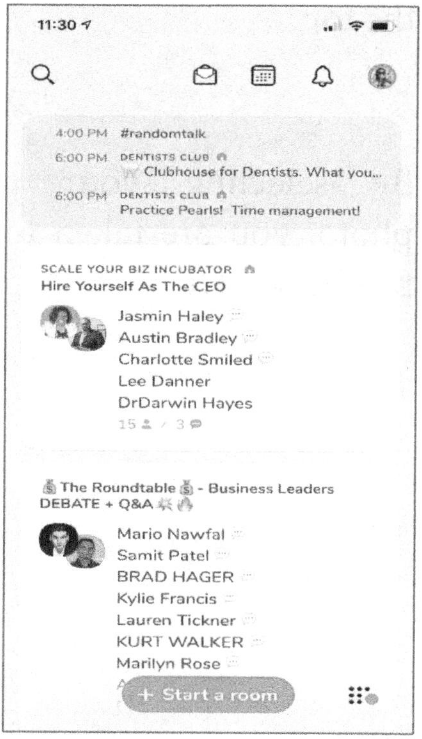

Let's now look at all the icons in the top menu bar.

I'll begin with your profile as this is the first thing that I want you to set up as soon as you join Clubhouse.

Your Profile

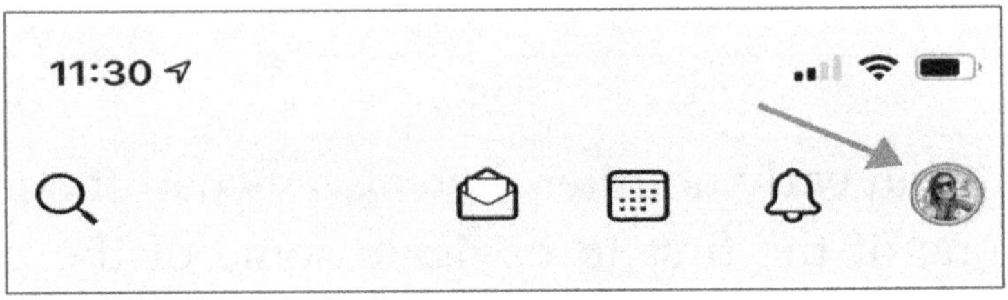

Click on your profile picture at the top.

By selecting your profile photo, you are taken to your profile screen.

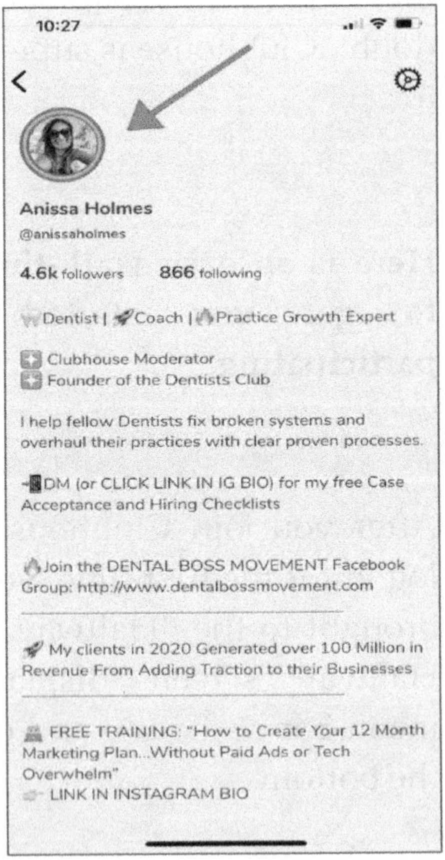

Here you can click on your profile photo to upload or change your photo.

Use a photo that shows off your face and unique personality. Select one with less of a busy background, or remove the background and add a pop of colour that makes you stand out in a crowd.

Go to Chapter 7 (Profile Photo Hacks for Dentists) to learn how you can do this by using remove.bg.

I also used canva.com to add a border around my photo to make it pop. I wanted to draw your attention. Did it work?

Under your profile photo, you will see your username.

Make sure you are absolutely sure about the name you choose to use. Clubhouse only gives you one opportunity to change your name.

To change your username, simply click on your current username, and a new window will give you access to make that change.

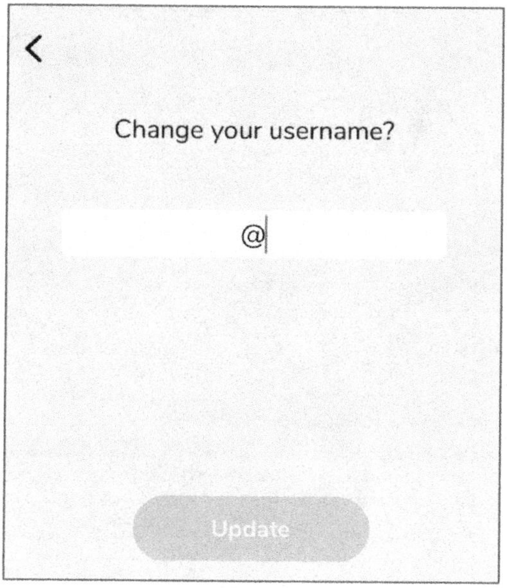

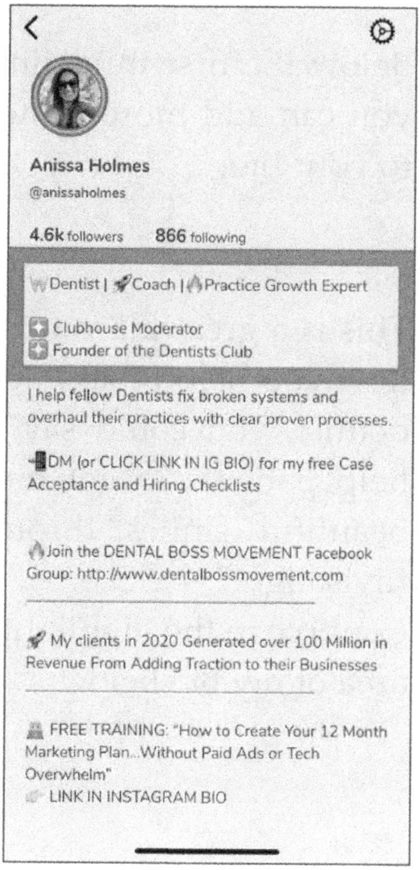

Your Bio

Next, we look at your bio.

Your bio is where you get to say what you want others to know about you. Note, the first three lines of your Clubhouse bio are the first information others get to see before choosing to read more. Here is an example of mine. Notice how I stated what I do and how they could benefit from me.

Below the first three lines, you can add more content to your bio.

This is a great place to say how you help others. As a dentist, you could say, "I help patients to get more beautiful smiles through Invisalign." See an example in the highlighted area of my bio below:

You can also add one or more call-to-actions (CTAs) to your bio.

A CTA is a direct call or request for the reader to take the action specified. Below I have called persons to DM and click for a free case acceptance and checklist and join the "Dental Boss Movement" on Facebook.

You could also add a few significant accomplishments. The image below shows how I added mine.

Adding your location is another cool connection hack because your bio is searchable. So, naming your location (city and state) will help people in your community find and connect with you.

Remember, emojis are also searchable. Adding them is an incredible way to separate your content and add a little style to your bio.

Check out how I used emojis in my bio (especially the tooth emoji beside Dentist):

The following bio "must-do" is, adding your link so that people can connect with you off the platform.

Presently Clubhouse allows you to add your Instagram and Twitter links to your bio. DMs are not available at this time. So, make sure you add your links and get ready to connect on and off Clubhouse.

Followers and Following

From your bio screen under your username, you can see the number of people following you and the number of people you follow.

Scroll to the bottom of your bio to see a list of your followers.

To follow persons who follow you, click the "Follow" button to the right of their names.

Settings

Now that your profile is completed, let's select your "Settings" options.

To do that, select the gear button at the top of your profile.

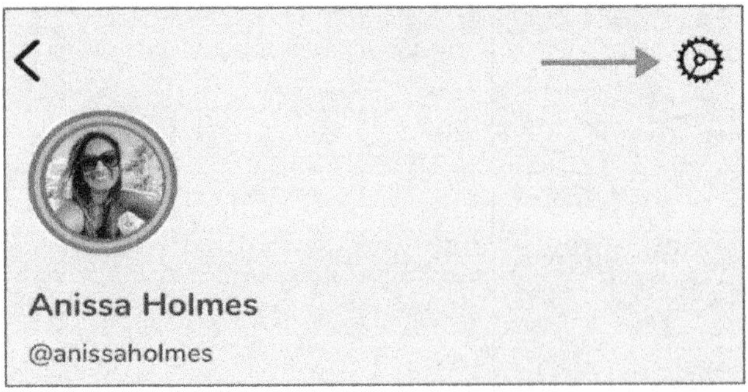

On the Settings screen, you will find notifications, interests, and Instagram/Twitter options.

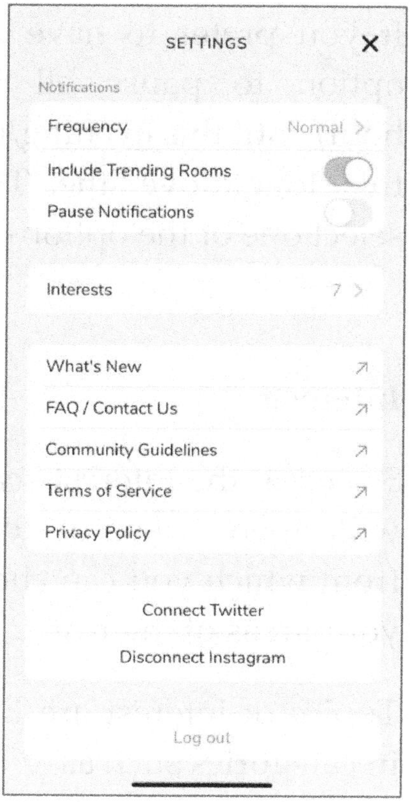

Notifications

At the top of the settings screen, you will see notification options.

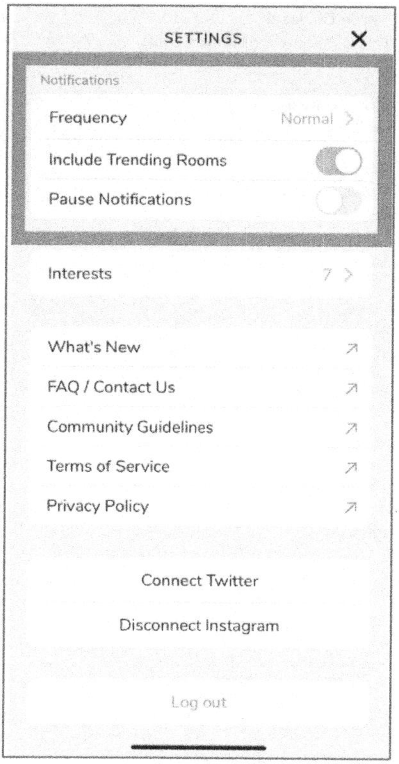

The frequency option allows you to choose how regularly you get notifications. The app sets your notification frequency on "normal." However, you can select the arrow to the right if you wish to change it.

If you prefer to have zero notification, you have the option to pause all incoming notifications for an hour/until this evening/until morning/ for a week. To do this, toggle over the "Pause Notifications" button, and select one of the options provided.

Interests

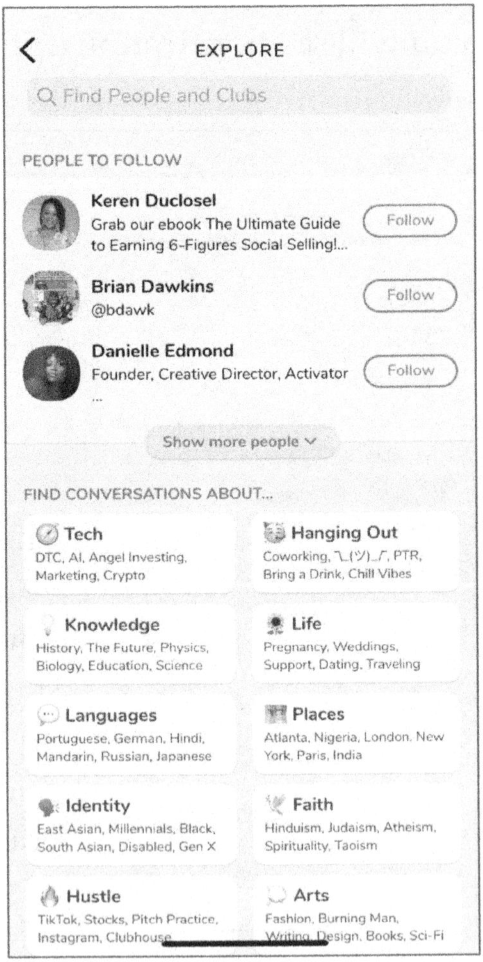

Selecting the interest screen will open a list of topics from which you can choose your areas of interest.

Topics of interest are listed in categories such as

- Life
- Identity
- Faith
- Hustle
- Places
- Hanging Out
- Entertainment
- Wellness
- Knowledge
- Sports

- Languages
- Arts
- Tech

By selecting an interest from one of the categories, you are automatically notified when related rooms are opened.

If you ever need to contact Clubhouse's admin or see their Terms of Service, this is where you would go:

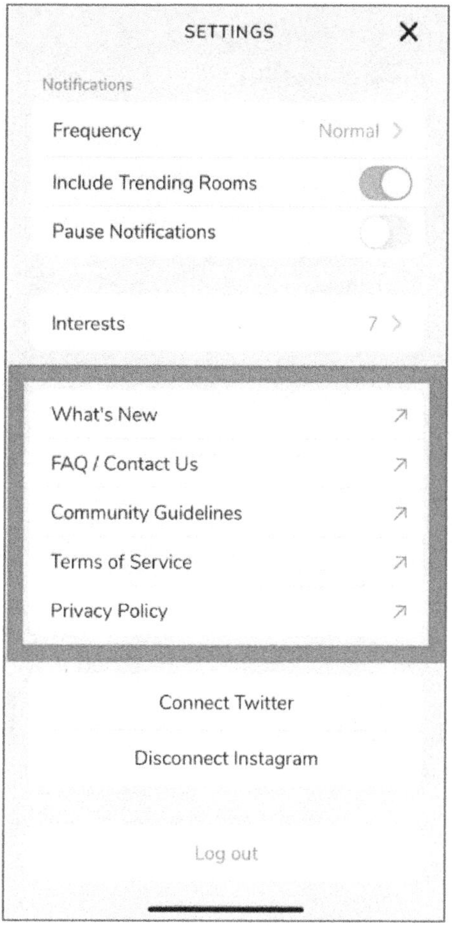

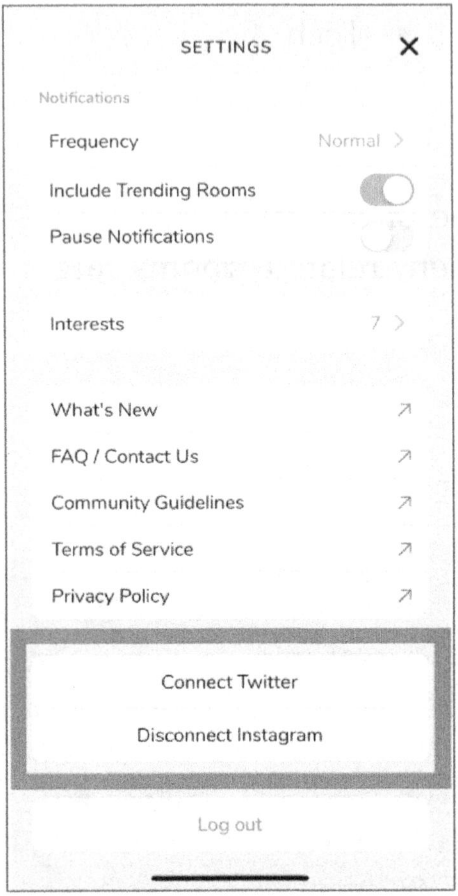

To the bottom of the "Settings" screen are Instagram and Twitter update options. Here you can change/update your social media link(s) in your bio.

Notification Bell

At the top of your "Profile" screen, you will see the "Notification Bell." The bell indicates when there is an activity that may interest you.

Activity

By selecting the "Notification Bell," you will be taken to the "Activity" screen.

The "Activity" sheet will display activities linked to your account such as, invites to rooms, scheduled rooms, opened rooms, etc.

If persons on your phone contact list joined Clubhouse, they would be listed in the activity section. You will also see the "Follow" option to follow them.

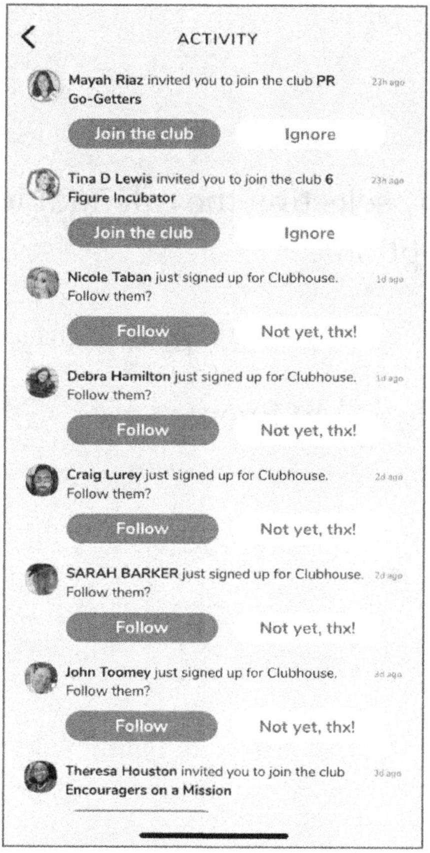

The Calendar

At the top of your profile page, you will also find the "Calendar" icon.

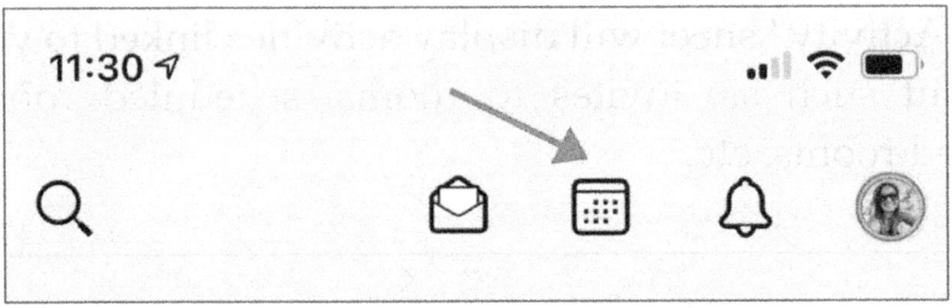

By selecting the calendar icon, you are given two primary options.

- Upcoming for You
- My Events

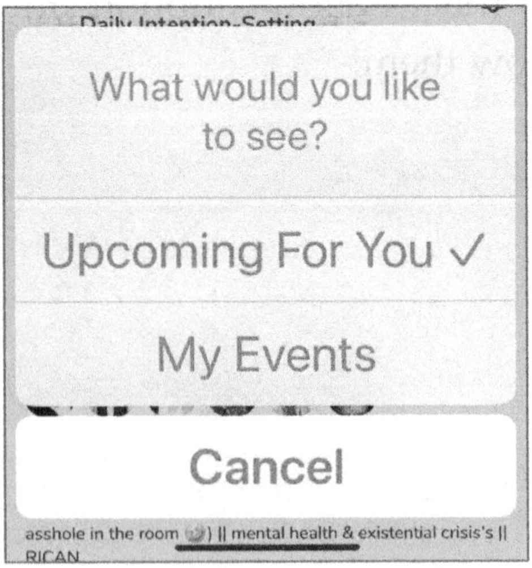

Upcoming for You

By selecting "Upcoming for You," a page will open showing all scheduled events (rooms) based on the people and clubs you follow and the interests you selected.

My Events

By selecting "My Events," a page will open showing all rooms/events you have scheduled and events you are scheduled to moderate or speak at.

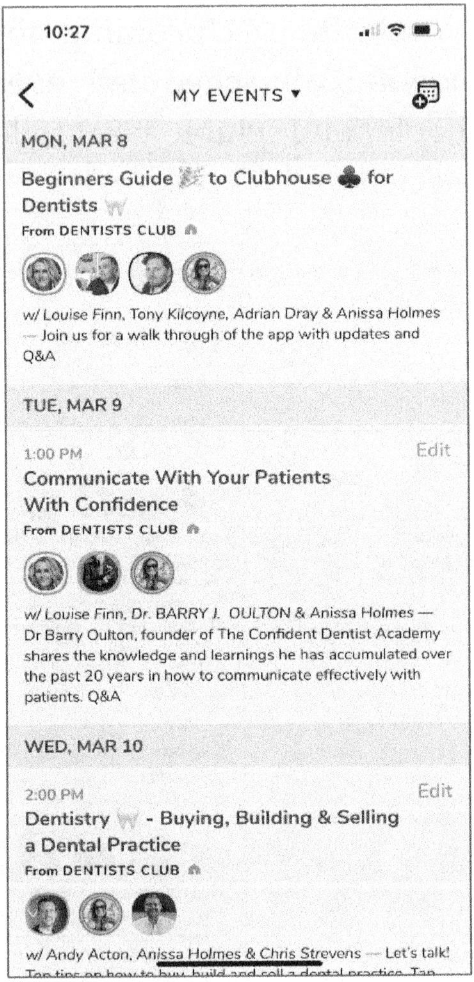

Pro Tip:

If you are on the "Upcoming for You" page, select the dropdown arrow to the right to see the calendar options.

How to Schedule an Event

The calendar is also used to schedule rooms and clubs.

To schedule an event, go to the calendar and select "My Events" from the options provided.

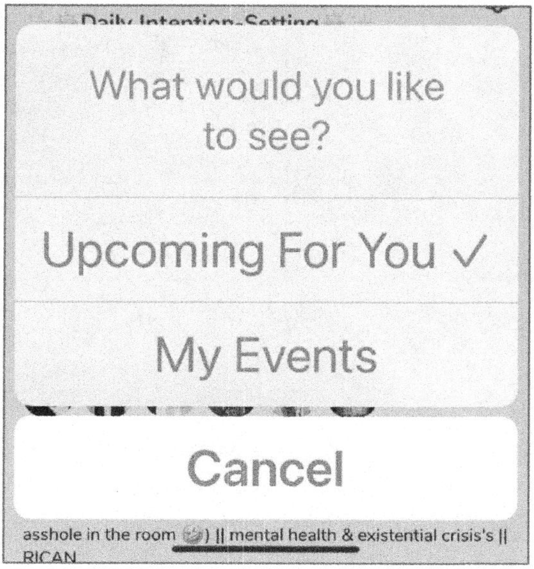

From your "My Events" page, click on the calendar icon at the top right. You will be taken to a page to create your event.

You will be required to fill in the event name, a co-host (optional), the date and time, and the event's description.

If you are hosting the event/ room within a club, you can note that as well.

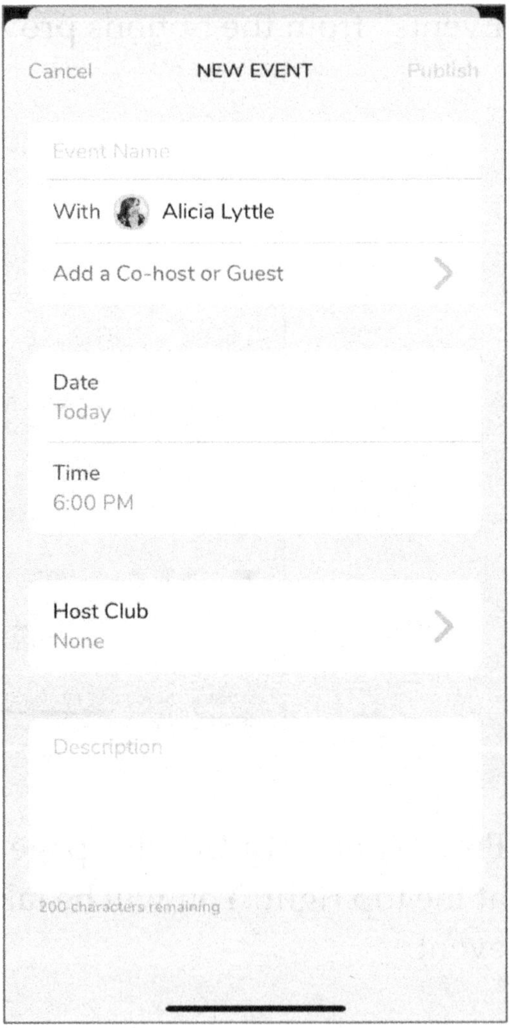

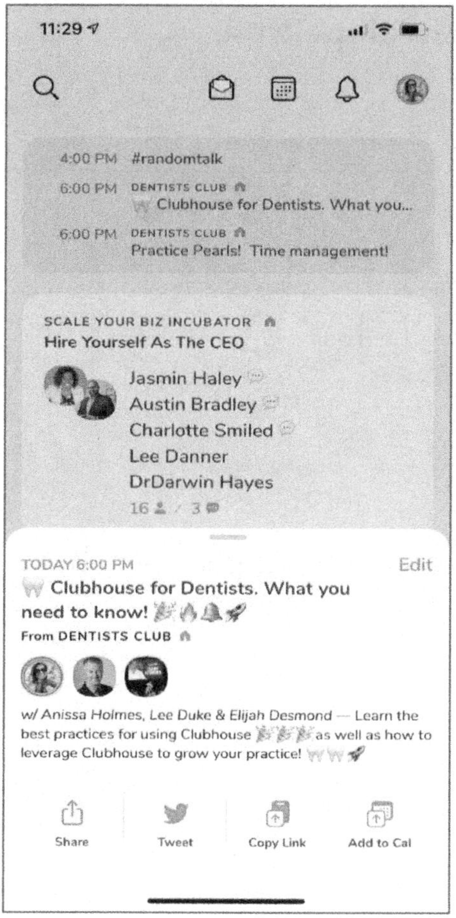

Once you have scheduled your event, you can invite people by clicking on the event to see invitation/ sharing options to "Share," "Tweet," or "Copy Link."

If you clicked on an event that you did not schedule, you would also see the "Add to Calendar" option.

How to Send an Invite - The Envelope Icon

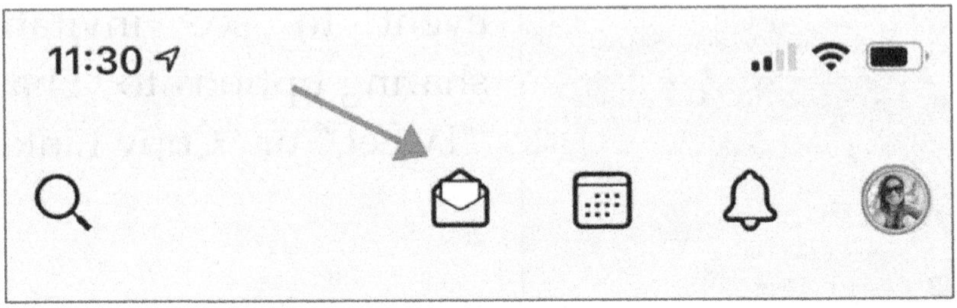

By clicking on the envelope icon, you get to see how many invites you have.

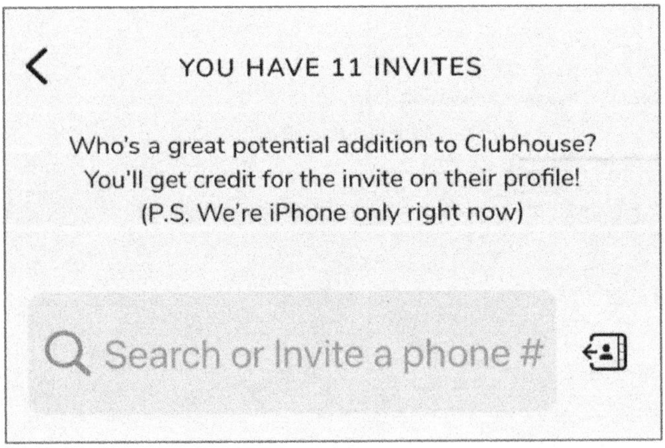

Search the contact list displayed for the person you want to invite.

Pro Tip:

To avoid wasting precious invites, confirm if the person (you want to invite) has an iPhone.

How to Find People on Clubhouse - The Explore Icon

By selecting the explore icon, you can find people and clubs you wish to follow.

Type in the name of the person you wish to find, and the page will show the search results. In the example below, my friend @AliciaLyttle searched for my name on Clubhouse.

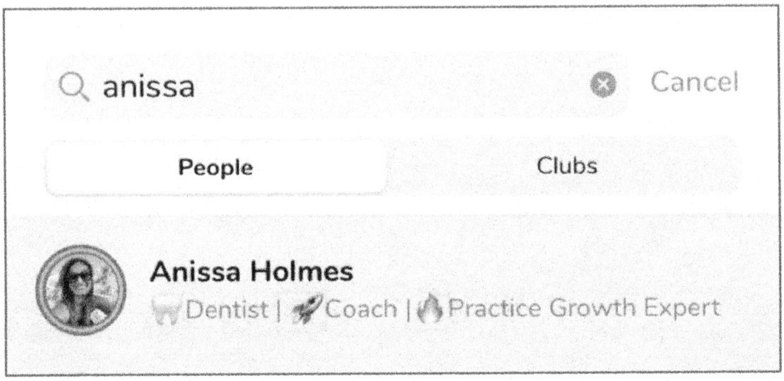

If you want to find a club, select "Clubs." Then, type in the name or topic related to the club you want to see.

In this example, I typed "dentist" in the search window. The results page listed a few dentists related clubs.

I selected the "Dentists' Club," which opened the page showing the club title, icon, description, members and followers.

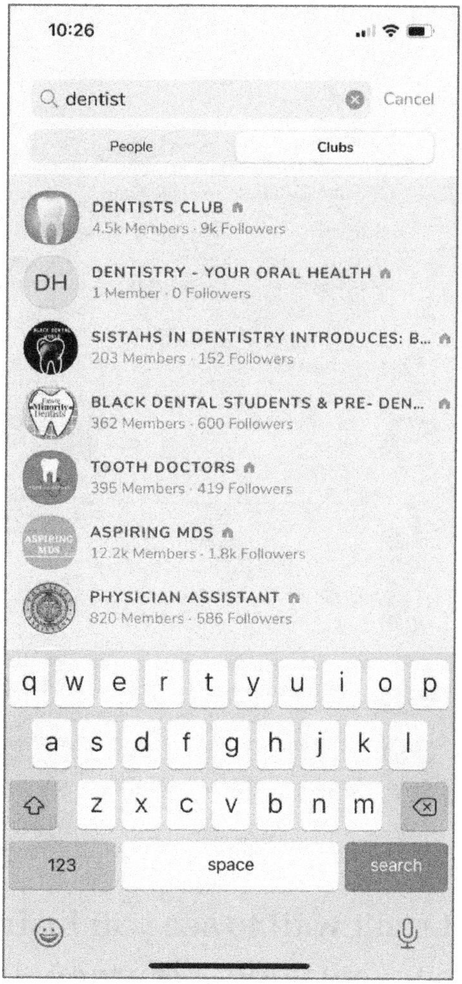

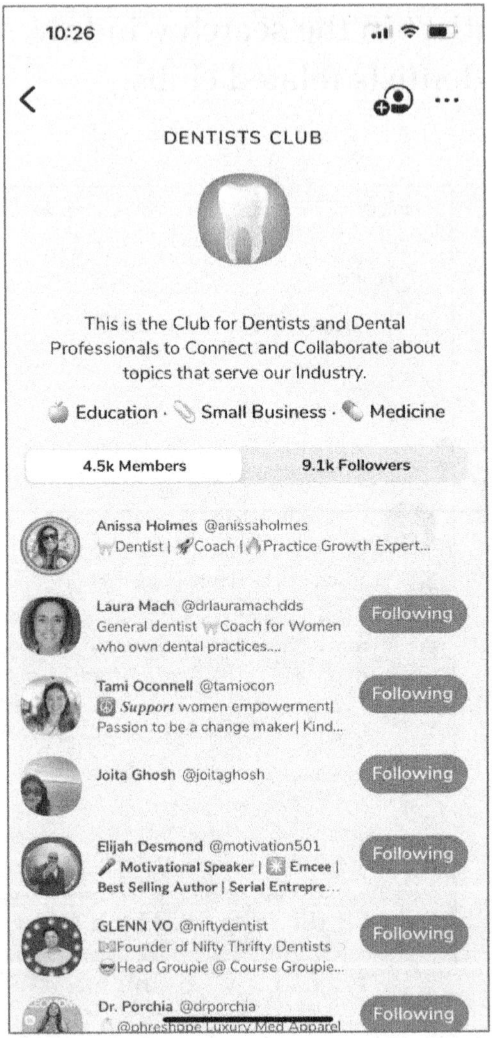

I invite you to join Clubhouse and follow our Dentists Club to connect and collaborate with other dental professionals.

Once you are following, you will have the opportunity to become a member of the club. As soon as you are a member, you are welcomed to start rooms.

I can't wait to see you inside Clubhouse. It's going to be an amazing journey—connecting, learning, and collaborating.

Chapter 9
Rooms Vs Clubs

On Clubhouse, clubs and rooms create the hub for connection, conversations, and collaboration.

Clubs

Like the clubs we joined when we were in school, a Clubhouse club is a community created around a common interest. Clubhouse members can follow a club at any time, based on their interests.

How to Follow and Become a Member of a Club

To ensure you follow a community of like-minded people, use the Explore feature to find the clubs that represent your areas of interest. When you click on a club from the search results, you will see the club's description and an option to follow the club you prefer. Currently, you cannot request to join a club. However, by following a club, the administrators have the option to make you a club member. You may even get the opportunity to create rooms within that club. For example, if you are a member of the Dentists Club, you can create a room to discuss cosmetic dentistry for kids, etc.

To follow a club, select the Explore icon from the profile page.

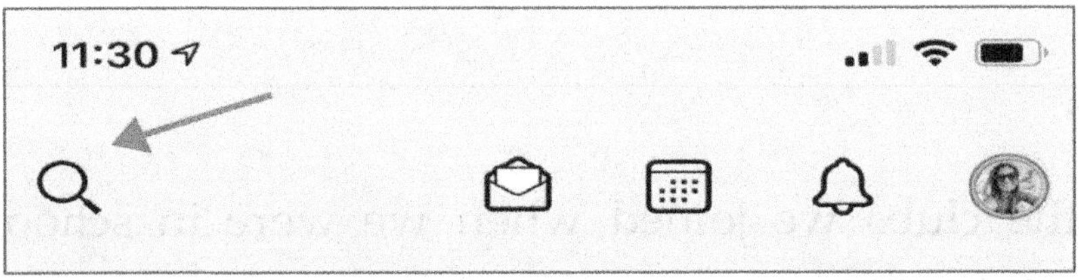

By selecting it, you will be shown a page to search for people and clubs.

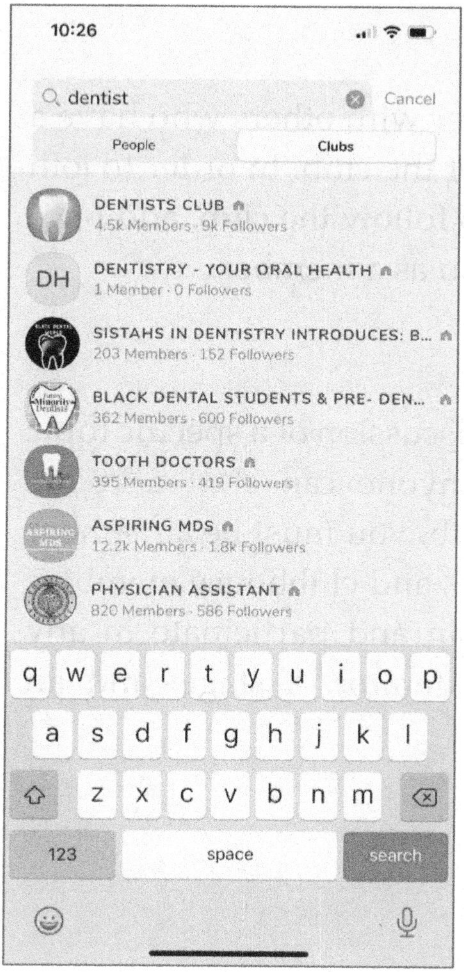

Type the name of the club or area of interest.

Following clubs give you access to meaningful discussions around your interests. For example, if you are interested in real estate and join or follow a club on real estate, you will receive a notification whenever the club is having a discussion.

So, as soon as you join Clubhouse, use the search feature based on your areas of interest (for example, dentist, music, soccer, etc.), so you can be a part of a community and have discussion rooms open up to you. There you can share and gather knowledge.

Clubs

Clubs are a great place to gather with others who have a common interest in the topic of the club. In order to join a club, you will first request to follow the club, and once done so, the admin can add you as a member.

Rooms

A room is a space created for discussion of a specific topic about a common interest. Anyone can start a room. However, to do so within a club, you must be a member of the club. All rooms are open, and clubhouse members have an open invitation to join and participate in any room. All rooms have a moderator, a stage, and an audience.

The Moderator

A moderator manages all the activities in a room on Clubhouse. The moderator is expected to steer the panel and audience into a meaningful conversation.

The Stage

By tapping on a room, you will immediately enter the room and are first taken to the audience. Only people speaking in the room are on stage. Pictures with the green "star" icon indicate who is a moderator in the room. If someone is speaking, you will see an outline around their picture.

Pro Tip:

Update your app settings, so you always automatically enter a room muted.

The Audience

Scroll past the stage; you will see the audience. All the member who are not speaking or moderating are listed in the audience area.

Chapter 10
Join Our Club
(The Dentists Club)

As a dental professional, you may be asking, "How can I find our community?" You are not alone; I was faced with the same question when I just joined Clubhouse.

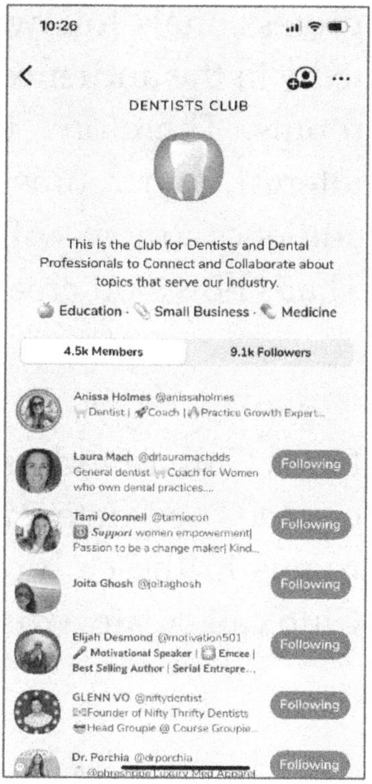

At that time, there were not many dental professionals on the app. I had a hard time finding discussion rooms related to dentistry. So excited, I decided to create a club for dentistry—the Dentists Club.

The Dentists Club is for dentists and dental professionals to connect and collaborate on topics that serve our industry. The vision is to give club members a voice and an opportunity to be identified as an expert. Club members can create discussion rooms and leverage the opportunity by having other dental professionals join to discuss various related topics.

On Clubhouse, what we see on our accounts is based on who we are following. If we do not have many dental professionals following us, not many persons are likely to be in the audience when we choose to start discussion rooms. Therefore, it is vital that we follow clubs of interest, join rooms, and follow people who are in the audience (they will follow back for the connection). That's how you create a community!

Note: Club founders set the parameters for the club they create. They determine if members are allowed to start rooms in the club or not. All members of the Dentists' Club can create a discussion room.

Why Join

This club is so powerful for all of us. It allows us to build and leverage our community. Now, it is so much more than joining a club. We can create rooms where we discuss clinical dental topics or rooms where we simply hang out with our people at the end of a long workday. Yes, we have had rooms like that :) The beauty about this is that, when we get talking, people with a common interest can create a room to discuss further the subject that started by simply hanging-out. The best part is that our club permits all members to start discussion rooms. (I say "our club" because it's our club, created for us).

The club has several thousand members currently. Not only does that give you a fantastic start to making connections, but it also creates endless possibilities for discussions and collaborations.

Follower or Member of a Club

To qualify to become a member of any club, you must first become a follower (as detailed in Chapter 9).

- To join a club, you need to search for your topic of interest (for example, dental clubs).
- The search results will show clubs related to the topic you searched (for example, surgical club).
- By clicking on any club from the results list, you will see the club description and an option to follow the club. Club administrators are notified once you choose to follow a club.
- Club administrators then choose to accept you as a club member. A vetting process is often used to aid their decision.

The Vetting Process

Club administrators vet the profiles of club followers to determine if they will accept a new follower as a member of the club. The club's dental professionals appreciate the vetting process because if they are starting rooms for members only, they know everyone has been confirmed to be a dental professional via the selection process.

Our vetting process involves looking at the followers' bios and social media connection. That helps to validate that the person is a dental professional—hygienists, team members, dental students, dental coaches, dental consultants, dental speakers, dental companies, etc.

Another feature is that as a club member, you can invite others into the club. While in a club, select the ellipsis (three dots) to the top right of the club's page. You will be taken to a page to search your clubhouse or your contacts for people to invite.

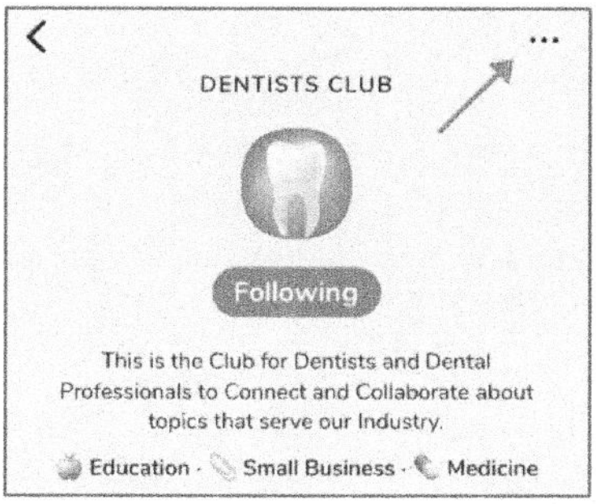

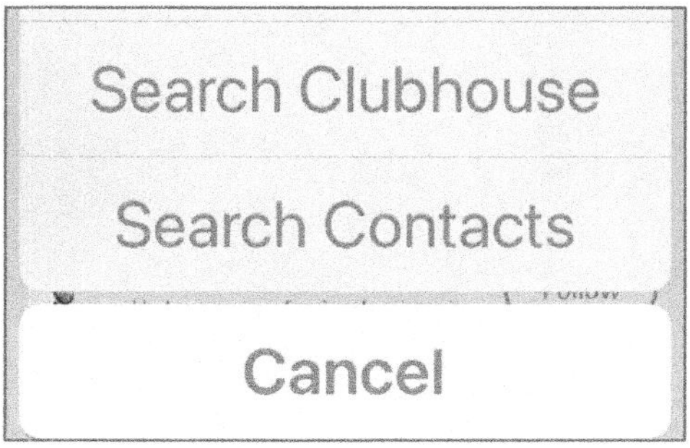

How Bio Impacts Membership

Remember earlier I mentioned that your bio is that second chance to make a first impression? Well, on the matter of vetting, it is the only opportunity to make that impression. Therefore, you must craft your Clubhouse bio to provide the relevant content to get you memberships into the clubs you choose.

As a vibrant community member, you have a voice and the ability to create rooms. That right there is community conversations toward collaborations!

Chapter 11
How Are Others Growing Their Dental Practices On Clubhouse?

It is incredible how our Dentists Club is growing, and even more mind-blowing is how dental professionals are using Clubhouse to grow their businesses. Below are a few stories of the real power of Clubhouse connections, conversations, and collaborations.

At the Dentists Club, we started a room discussing "How to grow your dental practice." In that session, we discussed marketing through Facebook lives and information videos.

After the discussion on Clubhouse, one of my students transferred the Facebook strategy by starting a room. Clubhouse members following her immediately joined the discussion, where she shared valuable dental information and answered their questions. She used before and after images to engage her audience and invited them to contact her directly for further support or click the scheduling link in her profile. As soon as the room ended, five people contacted her practice to make an appointment.

That was a win for her because she used the power of her voice, where the right people were listening. They heard her voice, and she gave them the option to contact her and schedule an appointment. Again, the power of Clubhouse!

Pro Tip:

Another great option is to add your online booking link. An easy and efficient virtual appointment booking app is calendly.com. Calendly allows patients to select their preferred times based on your availability and theirs. It also seamlessly links and updates your planner and Zoom accounts.

Add your link to your profile and constantly remind your audience to use it to make their appointments online. If your scheduling link is too long, here is an amazing hack to shorten or create your link.

- Shorten your link by using bitly.com. Bitly.com will allow you to create a short-customized link.

Chapter 12
Best Practice Moderator Tips For Running & Growing Clubhouse Rooms

A moderator manages all the activities in a room on Clubhouse. The moderator determines who gets into the room, who is allowed on stage (to speak), and in what order members of the audience get to speak. A Moderators can also assign moderator status to other persons on the stage. All moderators have the authority to remove someone from a room and decide when a room is closed.

Here are some tips and best practices for Clubhouse moderators:

- **Moderate Individually or Collaboratively**

Decide if you will moderate a room by yourself, with others, or both. I have found that both present different benefits.

Moderating with others opens the opportunity for future collaborations and enables you to serve the audience better. You could consider collaborating with colleagues who may be more knowledgeable regarding a specific subject than you. For example, if you and a few colleagues hosted a room on dental laser treatment, you would gain more knowledge on the subject.

Another amazing benefit of having a collaborative panel is that you can leverage having multiple moderators to grow your rooms. In a room, moderators are usually on stage, which means that the more moderators a room has, the more persons are notified and prompted to join the room. That creates the opportunity for a bigger audience and more connections. That said, be sure to choose your co-moderators wisely; they will also get to hold the controls of your room.

- **Be Clear about the Topic**

Decide on the topic you are going to discuss. Stick to that topic and ensure that you guide the discussion around that subject matter. Note, however, that persons allowed on stage may also introduce a new topic to the conversation. It is your responsibility to ensure that the primary topic remains the subject. After all, the people who joined the room are there to hear about the primary topic.

Depending on the extent and depth of discussion you have planned, it is essential to identify relevant sub-topics that could be raised.

- **Reiterate the Clubhouse Rules**

New people are always joining Clubhouse (though not yet public at the time this book was written). Thus, it is imperative to always go over the rules for the sake of your audience, new or returning. When a person is new to Clubhouse, a party hat emoji is shown next to their profile photo.

Pro Tip:

Always remember to welcome new members and tell them how to join the stage.

- **Stage or Audience**

Decide if you want to leave persons on stage/at the top, so they get to continue speaking, or if you're going to move them down into the audience after they've had an opportunity to talk. If you are moderating as a teacher in a room, you may want to move people into the audience once they have spoken. Conversely, you may be co-presenting with a team of experts, and the discussion requires that they remain on stage. Either way, you can't be wrong, do what works for you!

Start a room!

Experience the app!

Make connections! And . . .

Have lots of fun!

- **Give Your Listeners More Value-added Conversations**

By inviting listeners to follow you as a speaker, they are not just being notified when you open rooms; you are also inviting them to become club members. That gives them access to more value-added conversations.

When someone is following you as a speaker, they can choose to get notifications. Likewise, you can get notifications when someone you follow is speaking.

Go into their profile, and select the notification bell to the right of their profile photo.

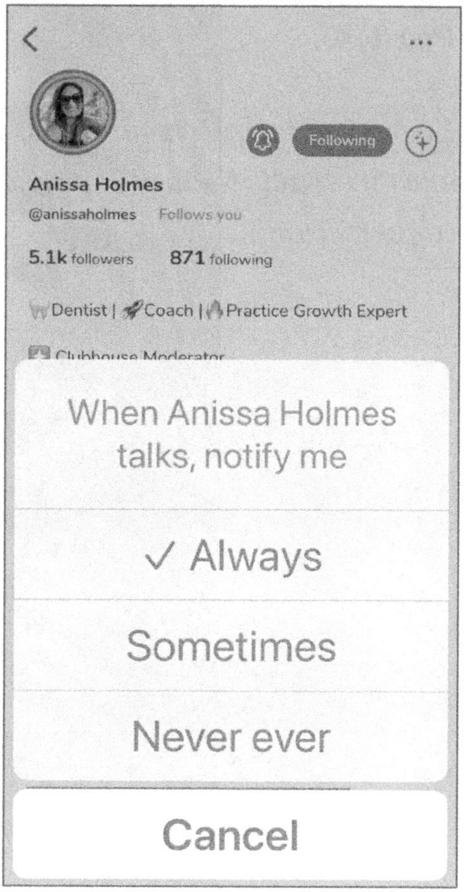

In this example, my friend Alicia went to my profile. Here she can choose to get notifications when I speak.

One other amazing feature of Clubhouse is that you can invite others into the club as a club member. As dental professionals, this feature allows us to continue connecting, collaborating, and building the community.

Pro Tip:

Every ten to fifteen minutes, remind the audience of the topic and instruct them to ping/invite their friends to join the conversation.

Chapter 13
Community Guidelines/Rules

Clubhouse is designed to foster community, connection, and conversation. The app's culture also encourages people to connect offline, which, for our industry, is very different from what happens on other social platforms.

Clubhouse, at its simplest, allows groups of people to hang out after a long day. For some users, it is primarily a place to get answers and not necessarily a place to sell or pitch services. For me, it is a place to show up and add value.

For me, it doesn't get better than that!

Since joining Clubhouse, I have started a club, opened and moderated many rooms, spoke on several panels, and sat in many audiences. From those experiences, I have listed a few points that will help you as you connect, share and learn.

1. To get the best personal experience out of every room you join, make sure you are clear about the questions you want to ask.

2. Write down your question in the most straightforward and concise way.

3. Focus on your question's purpose, so you do not leave the room without getting your question answered.

4. Ask your question exactly how you wrote it and allow the speaker to answer.

5. You do not need to share everything about your professional activities; that information is in your bio. Sticking to the discussion subject will compel persons to look at your bio.

Chapter 14
5 Things I Learned In My First 24 Hours On Clubhouse

1. This Platform Is About Connecting People

Can you find a better app where people connect, have conversations, continue conversations and forge collaborative relations than Clubhouse? Clubhouse does not simply connect people; it connects people with the intent to add value. To create the best experiences (for individuals, groups, professionals, industries, etc.), Clubhouse allows people to connect based on common interests, geographical locations, professional specializations, age groups, and professional and personal needs, etc.

2. The Most Brilliant Minds are on Clubhouse

"I remember joining a room and getting my questions answered by Damon John, free of cost! So, if you have questions and need answers, Clubhouse is one of the best places to be. There you will find experts, professionals, veterans, leaders, policymakers, and more speaking in rooms, answering questions, and collaborating.

3. I Need a Notebook

The value-added in every discussion room must have been a royal shock to everyone as it was to me when I just joined Clubhouse. I was learning so much; I had to start taking notes. So, though I was all ears, I decided I needed to write down what I learned.

4. Mute My Mic When I Go on Stage

It's a good thing I am a quick learner because this lesson came quite quickly after I joined. I had entered a room on my way home in traffic, and my mic was on, but I didn't notice. By the time I was home, I was on stage greeting the audience with the reggae ringtone of my other phone and my dog trying to say hello. (I pictured myself on a real stage, with my hand over my mouth thinking . . . OMG, what just happened?). Thank goodness the moderator was quick on his toes; he muted me and moved on to another member until I was ready.

6. Clubhouse Is a Fantastic Hangout Spot/App

After a long day's work, what better place to be than with friends sitting around the fire pit. The first time it hit me that we were just hanging out was one evening when I hopped out of the tub to join a room in the Dentists Club. We had no specific dental topic; we just shared about our day and how we are balancing work with personal life. It was so much fun; I felt I was in the company of friends who truly understood and could relate to what I was sharing. The best part is that we all got tips and strategies to make our days better by the time the room ended. How rewarding!

Chapter 15
Will Clubhouse Kill In-Person Dental Conferences?

Absolutely NOT!

Conferences in the past brought us physically together to meet, greet, share, connect, and much more. But let's face it, in-person seminars will never be the same, not after the pandemic. According to www.askwonder.com, the conference/meeting industry overnight went from over 1.8 million in-person meetings and events in the United States of America per year to only live-streamed events.

The natural desire for community, connection, and collaboration became the catalyst for the growth of many online meeting platforms and the unveiling of others. The pandemic brought us into a time where our voices were all we had, but not enough stages to share them. Then came Clubhouse, a place we could speak to each other, ask questions, and get answers.

For me and many others, Clubhouse could not have done a better job at connecting us, creating communities, and fostering collaborative opportunities.

What will a conference on Clubhouse do for us? Well, already, it has enhanced our conversational experiences. But l am seeing way more for Clubhouse than room and stages. I am foreseeing "Dental Conference Streamed Live on Clubhouse." The conference experience on Clubhouse would give power to learning from anywhere, for everyone. It will be a wealth of learning, in one place, for larger groups of people with equal interaction. Therefore, everyone has a voice—moderator, presenter, and every single member of the audience.

Why a room rather than Zoom? As I listen to live webinars on Zoom and compare my experience in a room on Clubhouse, I have come to realize that I would prefer to join a room rather than Zoom. Clubhouse eliminates finding a login link and registering. It provides a hassle-free way for us to connect, listen, learn.

Clubhouse is the perfect conversation balance between presenters and an audience. In-person conferences were planned around the presenters. It was all about the speech, the multimedia, the conference folders, and sales kits. Now, we can only speak to each other, so why not allow everyone to have a say? On Clubhouse, participation is almost a must. Rooms are designed to give every member a chance on stage to be a part of the discussion. Every member is a resource, and everyone is acknowledged on Clubhouse.

My questions were answered in real-time. On Clubhouse, you get to ask questions, and you get answers in real-time, all from the comfort of my home (or wherever you are). Now for the best part, whether off-stage or back-stage, you still get to connect after the discussion!

Clubhouse has, without a doubt, made the social distancing journey doable and winnable. It will not make in-person conferences extinct, but it has most definitely enhanced the opportunity to satisfy the need to connect, communicate and collaborate.

Regardless of the shift that Clubhouse, Zoom, and other platforms have created, people will always continue to crave the natural desire to connect in-person. Will they host a conference just to connect? You bet they will, perhaps right after the pandemic. When all is said and done, there is nothing like a genuine hug and a chat around the fire pit!

Chapter 16
Stay Obsessed, but Avoid Clubhouse Burnout!

When you find a good thing, it's hard to let it go (not even for a moment), and Clubhouse is an exceptionally good thing. So, the pressure is twice, if not thrice, as much to never miss out.

No need to ask if I am addicted to Clubhouse. The real question you should be asking is if Clubhouse is my only addiction.

The answer is no.

I am addicted to reading books. I am addicted to business/dental-related discussions. I am addicted to making connections with colleagues and clients. I am addicted to teaching and learning, and I am addicted to helping others. I bet this sounds like I am describing you, right?

So, no, Clubhouse is not my only addiction, but there is a reason why I am more addicted to Clubhouse than all those I mentioned. It's simple; Clubhouse is the all-in-one solution to all my other addictions. Clubhouse will not replace watching live webinars or reading physical books. However, it allows us connection and conversation, teaching and learning, promotion and collaboration . . . and so much more.

Remember, a good thing can become addictive. For some of us, it's the beach, our family, even our practices. But to enjoy the values in our addictions, we must sometimes turn down the flame to avoid losing the fuel.

If you are always on Clubhouse, you will end up consuming without outputting. Your lights will always be on, leaving you no time to replenish. To avoid burnout, join groups you truly have an interest in and listen, take notes and ask questions in rooms. Stay away sometimes to understand the content you've gathered; then recalibrate for another level of learning.

Above all, no matter what room you join, who you follow, or the connections you make, always remember that taking time away from Clubhouse to apply the learning you acquire is (must be) relevant to your BIGGER PICTURE! So, embrace the learning, gather the knowledge and enjoy the experience.

FAQs

1. **What is Clubhouse?**

Clubhouse is an invite-only, audio-based app where members can hop into themed rooms and talk to other members.

2. **Is Clubhouse a free app?**

Yes, but it is only currently available to iPhone users.

3. **Is Clubhouse available on Android?**

No, Clubhouse is currently only available to iPhone users.

4. **How does someone join Clubhouse?**

Clubhouse is an invite-only app. People can only join via an invite from an existing member.

5. **Does Clubhouse have a video component?**

No. The app is 100 percent audio-only.

6. **Can I record conversations on Clubhouse?**

No, recording conversations is expressly forbidden.

7. **How does the app work?**

Members are allowed to create or join rooms where live conversations take place. Persons can choose to participate or just listen. Recordings are not allowed, so make sure you are all ears.

8. **What is a club?**

Clubs represent a community of like-minded persons with common interests. Members have the option to follow and be considered for membership in clubs.

9. **What is a room?**

Rooms are started to facilitate discussions of a specific topic. Anyone on Clubhouse can start a room.

10. **What is the stage?**

The section in a room where speakers are shown.

11. What is the audience?

The section in a room where non-speakers can be seen.

12. Who is a moderator?

A moderator is someone who manages the discussion rooms. They allow members of the audience to enter the stage to speak. Moderators also regulate the tone, subject, and length of the conversations.

13. How do I increase my number of followers on Clubhouse?

If you want a bigger audience, the best way to get loyal followers is to have great conversations that offer value. Actively participate and represent yourself well in rooms.

Resources

- https://bitly.com/
- canva.com

QUICK REMINDER:

Remember to follow me on Clubhouse.

Anissa Holmes: @AnissaHolmes

Also, make sure you join the Dentists Club to share in the fun! https://www.joinclubhouse.com/club/dentistsclub

ONE LAST NOTE TO YOU

Remember, this book is dedicated to you, and I enjoyed sharing every word with you. But, if you don't show up, you won't have a chance to use your voice and add equal value like the smiles you give every day!

So, as you get ready to connect with me on Clubhouse, remember, it's a place where you can listen, learn and be an expert. This is your opportunity to let people hear your passion for your craft.

Listening on Clubhouse is comparable to closing your eyes and listening to a newly released YouTube video, where the musical arrangements and lyrical artistry of that song become your connection. So, whether you are discussing veneers or vinegar, Clubhouse will provide an audience for you to help others.

Here are a few takeaways I want you to remember:

Be ready to learn

Clubhouse is a virtual place of learning, literally. As I mentioned before, the knowledge you would have once paid thousands for is readily available in a room, on a stage, and at an event on Clubhouse. Not only have I been able to teach upcoming dental professionals, but I have also gathered a plethora of knowledge that even I (the veteran) have implemented into my business/practice. You, too, can leverage this app to grow your business by showing up, taking notes, and being ready to learn.

Get your message out there

People are on Clubhouse, and right now, they are listening. Getting new patients resides in getting your message in front of them. So, since people are coming to Clubhouse for information, why not give it to them? You will grow your network and business in a single effort. Listeners will begin to see you as the authority and want to hear more from you. This is free marketing with mutual benefits. Whether you create a room or an event, theme it and let the discussions begin!

Help your colleagues

You can also help other dentists on Clubhouse.

Share Clubhouse tips with your colleagues. Discuss how they can craft their bios and word their titles. For example, adding your location to your bio and title, like "Dentists in Atlanta," will help get people from your area to find and follow you.

Start a room and share your knowledge and wisdom with your colleagues. If you have built several practices, you can get on stage and share your experiential knowledge and expertise in building thriving practices. On Clubhouse, the opportunity to share the knowledge you have doesn't require you to be the famous expert coach, consultant, speaker, lecturer, or a big name that everyone knows. Here you get to be the authority because you know.

You and I can be everyday dentists starting and leading discussions and sharing pearls with colleagues that helps others and expands our network. It also gives us that self-actualized satisfaction that we have added value to industry and people. How rewarding!

Serve your community/prospective patients

What's excellent about Clubhouse is that you can create your weekly room. People who are already looking for information have the opportunity to listen to you and get current information that will benefit them. These persons also have the power to invite their friends, family, and co-workers in your community to join the conversation (Since, there is no arm prompting them to invite a friend, go right ahead). Now, you have a marketing team because you gave them something that benefits them. Remember when I said that my practice has transitioned from service to service-relationships? This is precisely what I meant. The listeners with whom you have formed that bond will see you as more than and the expert, but someone they know and trust. That means, whenever they decide to or have a need to see the dentist, you are their go-to. They will not be price shopping or scouting other dentists on Google; they will come straight to you. You are also the first person they will recommend to anyone with a dental need or a question.

When they walk into the door, they will say they heard you on Clubhouse!

For food establishments, the line out the door sells every plate. It tells onlookers that the food is good there. A little from now, when patients walk into your practice and say they heard you on Clubhouse, you and your entire team will be elated. Job performance will shoot through the roof, and a sense of brand loyalty will define your service-relationships. That will inherently allow you to do more dentistry and elevate your practice into doing high-value/high-dollar procedures without ever having to think about discounts. So often, dentists have to decide to discount (because of the competition) their prices to get patients. The power to overcome the struggle with the competition is invaluable here. When a customer comes for the relationship and not just the service, the cost does not matter.

Help On-Stage and Follow Up Off-Stage

The app showcases you helping others live and onstage. From your radio show or weekly room, Clubhouse makes it possible for you to make yourself available to serve others on and off the stage. It's almost like you get to own a radio station, and you dictate the on-air time.

Facebook pages and Instagram accounts are outstanding, but there are some limitations. On a Facebook live, people can only type their questions, and almost all the time, they will not go in-depth with their questions. On Clubhouse, people can directly voice what is on their minds. For example, a person may ask, "My 13-year-old son broke a front tooth a few years now. Can he get an implant?" There you can also answer or even respond with follow-up questions and discussion. This does not happen so effortlessly on other platforms. Here, Clubhouse is facilitating awareness for many others while establishing you as an authority in the space.

If you have a sweet tooth, you will love that Clubhouse gives you the avenue to engage listeners off-stage. What I mean is that while you are on stage/on-air, other listeners benefiting from the information may choose to remain silent, book an appointment, or contact you directly. Remember, Clubhouse is always showing you off, and others will want to have you in their back pocket too. So, when you are hosting, always remember to remind your audience that they can contact you directly to ask questions. Nothing is as unique as a customer getting one-on-one service from a professional. The cherry on top is that you can even put your online scheduling link within the app. How amazing!

Share Business Management Skills

After all, we are in business to make money.

Other dentists on Clubhouse right now will agree that Clubhouse is a reliable place to market our practices, get patients, and book high-value procedures. That said, as practitioners and administrators, we have gained invaluable business knowledge via the Clubhouse interface. Running a business is not the same as fine-tuning one's technical skills. It takes practical business knowledge to make a business successful, whether we are selling veneers or vinegar. :)

I have listened to and shared the ins and outs of getting a dental practice off the ground and managing a dental practice. I have even heard value-added discussions on case acceptance, practice management, accessing financing for practice and clinical pearls, etc. The topics are endless . . .

As skilled practitioners, we need business knowledge to make our practice thriving. On Clubhouse, we can get free business knowledge; we can start a discussion around our business plans and get feedback. We can ask direct questions and get immediate responses from business experts and other experienced dental professionals. I guarantee you that for any question you can think of on dentistry or the business, there is someone who can answer you or someone creating a room about that exact topic. If the room does exist on the topic of your interest, create the room, and let the discussions begin.

I have been in rooms where the discussion was about (among other topics)

- How to build a great team;
- Facebook marketing versus Google marketing;
- Paid marketing versus non-paid marketing;
- How to grow your business from one location to five locations; and
- How to prevent burnout while trying to grow a business and have a family.

Above all, the most important part of dentists being on Clubhouse is the opportunity to get into the firepit and know that our community is here with and for us.

As I've always said, "in our pockets are friends and family and even our spouses, but in our back pockets, we have our community." Clubhouse allows us to have our community there, holding our hands and lifting us on a day, on the way, or as we need it. We can then continue to learn and grow together in a space where we are understood by each other.

Together we share real stories, share our voices, and bear our vulnerabilities, reveal the struggles and the solutions we have gone through. When you experience that connection, there is no turning back, and suddenly you realize you are not alone. You will realize that someone else's solution can become yours.

That's the power of Clubhouse!

Collaborate On-Line and Off-Line

Several conversations that started on Clubhouse have developed into collaborations for bigger discussion rooms. Larger discussions allow smaller groups to join and get more information, form larger networks, and generate more value.

For example, if you offer high-end cosmetic dentistry or you've mastered using Instagram to grow your business, you can connect (while in the discussion) with someone in the same space, even if they are on the other side of the world.

The connection sets you up for off-line conversations. Off-line conversations will enable sharing of information and collaboration on myriad ventures and opportunities. You would be surprised how collaborative efforts online can grow businesses.

The possibilities for synergy are endless, but what is truly remarkable is that Clubhouse has made it so easy for us to come together authentically. Our devices only separate us; it's the power of our voices that makes it so real. I literally feel like I am physically in the same room. We can be in these Clubhouse rooms every day (virtual rooms, a matter of fact), doing things we only get to do at two or three conferences annually.

Everything is happening in real-time. Sometimes so fast, the investment deals are made, and before you know it, a dentist is preparing to open a new location in a couple of weeks.

Interestingly, alliances with other dental coaches and consultants have helped to foster mutual professional respect for each other. We are now happy to share the stage with other pros and sit on panels. We now tag team to help and provide information to doctors, team members, and other associates.

Collaborating with other dental professionals on marketing activities helps us to collectively create powerful rooms of information for those who we all serve.

Clubhouse has had many pockets of surprises for me. Without even knowing, I have been connecting and building collaborations offline since I joined Clubhouse. In fact, I have had multiple accomplished dental companies (which heard me on Clubhouse) contact me to offer partnership and speaking opportunities. On Clubhouse, listeners can immediately bring other people who they feel need to hear my message into the room. CEOs have come into my rooms and said that they were pinged by someone else. Again, the power of Clubhouse!

Teach and Learn Practice 101 (Startup & Management)

Clubhouse is a place of learning where educators can thrive and share experiential knowledge and teach other professionals. They will always add value to dentists and dentistry.

We can certainly use many routes to educate others, such as being a speaker, hosting physical events, hosting webinars, and even Facebook lives. However, Clubhouse makes it simple and possible for you in 1, 2, 3:

1. Pick up your phone;
2. Start a room; and
3. **Start sharing.**

The Power of Clubhouse is that you can teach from just about anywhere—in your pajamas, sitting in the park, or walking your dog. There is someone who needs the wealth of knowledge you have, and you get the opportunity to connect and help others live and direct on Clubhouse. The best part is that you do NOT need to travel thousands of miles or be away from your family. You do not need to understand the technology of how to run a webinar.

I have been in rooms where aspiring practice owners are given practice 101 tips, covering topics such as, identifying the right location, negotiating leases, and marketing a new practice.

The opportunity lets you help others, and it showcases you as one knowledgeable on the subject. Thus, with the app, you can expand your service and business to others.

The more you serve, the more connections you make, the more collaborations you are a part of, the more you grow, and the more your business grows—and the cycle continues.

On Clubhouse, you can connect and grow a following of people who believe in you and want to learn from you; <u>and you never need to have an email list</u>.

***

Clubhouse has millions of members and is growing. It is the place people now go to get fast, free information on just about anything. This is your opportunity to show up, learn, teach earn and grow.

Your Notes

Your Notes

Your Notes

Your Notes

Your Notes

Your Notes

Your Notes

Your Notes

Your Notes

Your Notes

Made in the USA
Monee, IL
04 November 2026

67385873R00079